# CITIES OF ASIA

LIZ GOGERLY

ILLUSTRATED BY
VICTOR BEUREN

W
FRANKLIN WATTS
LONDON·SYDNEY

Franklin Watts

First published in Great Britain in 2021

by The Watts Publishing Group

Copyright © The Watts Publishing Group 2021

Credits

Artwork by Victor Beuren

Design: Collaborate Agency

Editor: Nicola Edwards

ISBN 978 1 4451 6887 6 (hb); 978 1 4451 6888 3 (pb)

Printed in Dubai

Franklin Watts

An imprint of

Hachette Children's Group

Part of the Watts Publishing Group

Carmelite House

50 Victoria Embankment

London EC4Y 0DZ

An Hachette UK Company

www.hachette.co.uk

www.franklinwatts.co.uk

# CONTENTS

# CITIES OF ASIA

**Welcome to Asia, the largest and most populated continent on Earth. This vast and exciting area measures 44,579,000 square kilometres, which is roughly 30 per cent of the land area of the planet. It's home to about 4.5 billion people, around 60 per cent of the world's population.**

The cities of Asia come in all shapes and sizes but they are often very big! The top six most populated cities in the world are in Asia. Shanghai, China, with more than 26 million people, is the world's most populous city. Beijing, China and Karachi, Pakistan are second and third respectively, with populations of more than 18 million each.

ANKARA

TEHRAN

ISLAMABAD

KATHMANDU

RIYADH

DUBAI

DELHI

Asian cities continue to grow in size. Perhaps that's why there are so many supertall buildings over 300 metres in height here; 18 of the 20 tallest buildings in the world are to be found in Asia. Burj Khalifa in Dubai in the United Arab Emirates is 828 m high and is the world's tallest building.

**Burj Khalifa**

People love to visit Asia's cities. Bangkok is the most popular tourist destination in the world. Singapore City; Tokyo, Japan; Kuala Lumpur, Malaysia and Seoul, South Korea are all top places to visit, too.

You will also find some of the world's best things to eat in Asian cities. Tokyo is one of the top places for fine dining. Street food is another highlight – it's fast, cheap and often delicious. Bangkok, Thailand; Tokyo; Hong Kong, China; Mumbai, India; Ho Chi Minh City, Vietnam and Beijing are known for serving up some of the best!

Asia has some of the longest and busiest metro systems in the world. Beijing has the busiest metro, with around 3.2 billion users whizzing round the city each year. Shanghai has the longest, and attracts over three billion customers a year. Some of the underground trains in Seoul have heated seats and internet services, making it possibly the world's most luxurious metro ride.

So pack your bags and don't forget your passport, as we explore some of the most fascinating cities in Asia.

TOKYO

SEOUL

BEIJING

SHANGHAI

DHAKA

HONG KONG

HANOI

MANILA

BANGKOK

SINGAPORE CITY

JAKARTA

One of the newest buildings in Beijing is the **CITIC Tower.** It got its nickname, the China 'Zun' Tower, because it looks like an ancient wine container called a zun. Building began in 2011 and it was completed in 2019. At 528 m high, the CITIC Tower is the tallest building in Beijing and the tenth tallest in the world.

The **China Media Group (CMG) Headquarters** almost looks like it's made of LEGO. Actually, it's quite a complicated design with two towers connected by a loop of horizontal sections. Locals call it 'big underpants' because of its strange shape! It has 51 storeys and was completed in 2012.

The **Beijing National Stadium** (the **Bird's Nest**) was built for the 2008 Beijing Olympic Games. The design was based on Chinese ceramics but it looks more like a bird's nest. Its huge roof is retractable and can be rolled back to make the stadium open to the sky.

# BEIJING
## CHINA

Welcome to Beijing, the capital city of the People's Republic of China. Beijing, also known as Peking, is one of the oldest cities in the world, dating back 3,000 years. Today, it is the world's most populated capital city, with nearly 22 million people living here. The skyline is filled with modern skyscrapers but there are many historic buildings to see too.

The modern world meets the old world at Beijing's **Forbidden City.** These beautiful pavilions were built during the Ming Dynasty, over 600 years ago. The city was so named because ordinary people were not allowed to enter – only the imperial family and their officials.

The best way to get around this city is on the **Beijing Subway**. It has 22 lines and is the second longest underground rail network in the world – the Shanghai Metro is number one.

# HISTORY

The history of Beijing goes back over 3,000 years. Long ago it was called Jin City. In 1403 the Yongle Emperor of the Ming Dynasty moved the royal seat to the city and named the new capital Beijing. The city has been the capital for most of its history. The People's Republic of China was established here in 1949. Since then the city has been modernised, but there are still old parts of the city left to explore.

# MONEY

In China the official currency is called Renminbi which means 'the people's money'. Units of currency are called yuan. Each banknote has a portrait of Mao Zedong (Chairman Mao) on it. He was the founding father of the People's Republic of China in 1949.

**Tiananmen Square**

# PLACES TO GO

**Tiananmen Square**

Beijing's Tiananmen Square is one of the largest city squares in the world. Tiananmen means 'Gate of Heavenly Peace' and a gate to the Imperial City was built here in 1415. The square you see today was built in 1651. People come here to visit the Mausoleum of Chairman Mao and the National Museum of China.

Tiananmen Square is famous for its military parades, political events and protests. Police always closely watch what is happening here. People go through security checks before they enter the square and cameras record everything!

# FOOD

**Peking duck**

Beijing is the best place in the world to eat Peking duck. Roast crispy duck is served with sweet bean sauce and pancakes. The dish was introduced to the city by royal emperors back in the thirteenth century.

**Jianbing**

Breakfast is a real treat in Beijing. Street vendors serve up delicious *jianbing*, which are pancakes stuffed with fried bread, spring onions and egg.

Jianbing

Peking duck

Jingshan Park

# THINGS TO DO

**Look for the Bell and Drum Towers**

These are symbols of old Beijing. Long before the skyscrapers, they were the tallest buildings in the city.

**Climb the hill in Jingshan Park**

A beautiful green space beside the Forbidden City, Jingshan Park has an artificial hill which you can climb to get fantastic views over Beijing, as well as of the Forbidden City itself.

**Visit the Temple of Heaven**

Construction of these religious buildings began in the fifteenth century around the same time as the Forbidden City. The highlight is the Hall of Prayer for Good Harvests.

Temple of Heaven

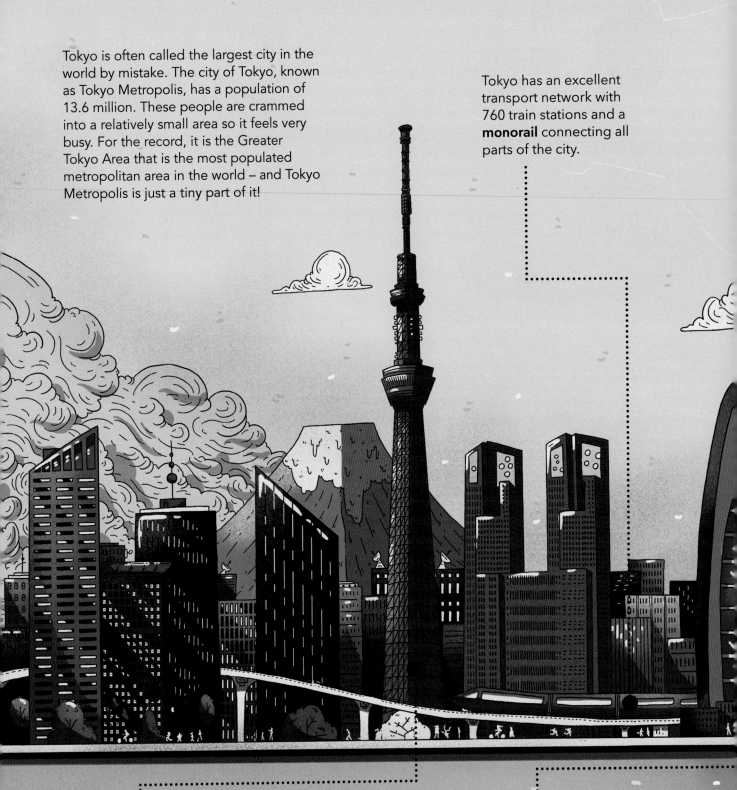

Tokyo is often called the largest city in the world by mistake. The city of Tokyo, known as Tokyo Metropolis, has a population of 13.6 million. These people are crammed into a relatively small area so it feels very busy. For the record, it is the Greater Tokyo Area that is the most populated metropolitan area in the world – and Tokyo Metropolis is just a tiny part of it!

Tokyo has an excellent transport network with 760 train stations and a **monorail** connecting all parts of the city.

At 643 m high, the **Tokyo Skytree** is the tallest tower in Japan. On its completion in 2012, it was the second tallest structure in the world.

People escape the busy streets by taking to the water. Cruises across Tokyo Bay in the **Himiko** and **Hotaluna** boats are trips like no other. The Himiko looks a little like a teardrop, while the Hotaluna could easily be a spaceship from the future.

# TOKYO

## JAPAN

The busy, buzzing streets of Tokyo are a place where the old world meets the new. From the top of the famous Tokyo Skytree tower, you can see the enormous, modern cityscape and its skyscrapers, with Japan's highest mountain, Mount Fuji, in the distance.

**Harajuku** is the place to see the extraordinarily colourful street fashions worn by local teenagers. People also head here to buy vintage clothes.

Tokyo hosted the **Olympic Games** in 1964 and was chosen to host the 2020 Games too. New sports such as surfing, sport climbing, karate and skateboarding were planned to be introduced in 2020.

# HISTORY

Four hundred years ago, Tokyo was a small fishing village. In 1590 a group led by a Shōgun, a military dictator, moved to the area and named it Edo. By 1867 Emperor Meiji had taken over from the Shōgun, renamed Edo Tokyo and turned it into Japan's capital city. Today, the Emperor of Japan lives at the Tokyo Imperial Palace.

# MONEY

The yen is the official currency of Japan.

# THINGS TO DO

### Experience Tokyo's passion for fashion

Tokyo is famous for its colourful and interesting fashions. People mix traditional dress with modern styles to create some amazing new looks.

### Try out a lovely loo

Tokyo toilets come in all shapes and sizes. Squat toilets are just holes in a porcelain base on the floor. Most people prefer washlets. These have heated seats and offer washing and drying functions – as well as playing music!

## FOOD

### Sushi paradise

Sushi is a Japanese national dish and Tokyo has the best – and the most – sushi bars in the world. There are believed to be around 3,620 sushi restaurants – which means you could visit a new one each day for nearly ten years!

### Big fish

Tsukiji fish market is the biggest seafood market in the world. Get up early to see the famous tuna auction. In January 2019 the owner of a Japanese restaurant chain paid a record £2.5 million for a giant tuna.

Sushi

## PLACES TO GO

Cherry blossom tree

### Green spaces

You can escape the noise of the city at Ueno Park or Inokashira Park. In spring people flock here to see the beautiful cherry blossom trees in bloom.

### Studio Ghibli

Over at Inokashira there is the Ghibli Museum where you'll find everything you ever wanted to know about the world-famous animation studio.

### Olympic venues

The 2020 Tokyo Olympic Games were planned to take place in around 30 venues around the city. The huge New National Stadium. completed in 2019, can seat 68,000 spectators.

### Tokyo International (Haneda) Airport

This is the third busiest airport in the world. It has so many restaurants and shops it feels more like a huge shopping mall than an airport. From the open-air observation deck you can watch the planes take off.

The Jakarta skyline is packed with skyscrapers and many more 'supertalls' (see page 4) are planned for the city in the future.

Now the tallest building in Indonesia is Jakarta's **Gama Tower**. It was topped off (completed) in 2016 and measures a whopping 310 m. The restaurant on the 51st floor offers the best bird's eye view of the city.

**Wisma 46** is easily recognised because of its curiously curved spire. At 262 m, Wisma was the tallest skyscraper in Indonesia until 2015.

The impressive **Icon Towers** is a complex of two skyscrapers that opened in 2019.

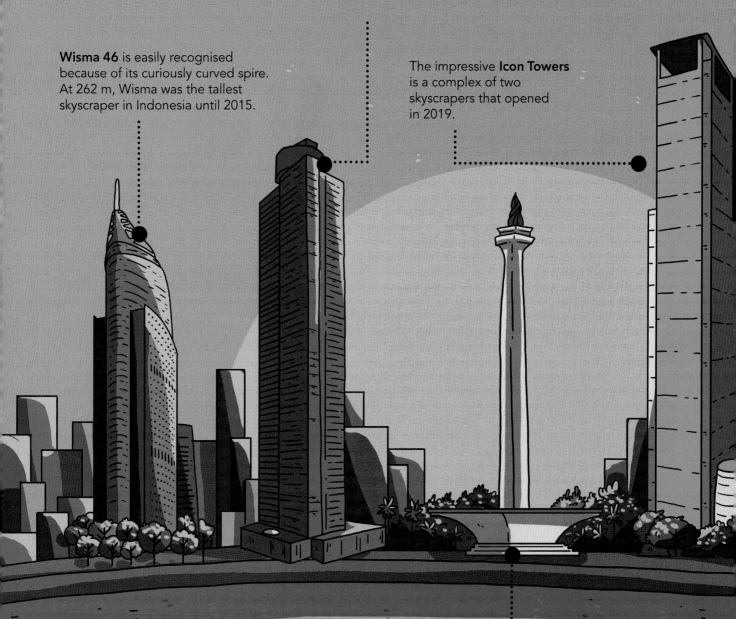

**Merdeka** (meaning Independence) **Square** is one of the largest city squares in the world. It is partly paved but people love coming here for its green spaces. At the weekend the fields are packed with people playing volleyball or badminton. The trees in the gardens provide shade from the hot sunshine. Children enjoy the sounds and the water from the musical fountain.

# JAKARTA
## INDONESIA

*Selamat datang!* You've arrived in Jakarta, the capital of the Republic of Indonesia. Situated in the northwest of the island of Java, this huge, sprawling city has a population of around ten million people. Javanese, Balinese, Chinese and European people call this city home so it has a richly diverse and exciting feel.

It's hard to believe you are in the Indonesian capital as you wander around the cobbled streets in the old town of **Batavia**. Many of the buildings here were built in the seventeenth century by Dutch colonists.

In Jakarta you are never far from the beep of car horns and wailing sirens. It has some of the most congested roads in the world. It is claimed that, on average, Jakartans spend 63 hours stuck in traffic each year!

One of the best ways to explore the centre of this busy city is by bike. Tourists can also take a free city tour bus.

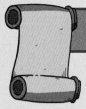

## HISTORY

Jakarta has a long history that goes back to the fourth century. From 1610 to 1942 it was occupied by the Dutch and was known as Dutch Batavia. In 1942 the Dutch surrendered the city to the Japanese. The next years were unsettled, but in 1949 Indonesia gained full independence and the city was renamed Jakarta. Since the 1950s the city has grown and developed into a thriving modern capital.

## MONEY

The local currency is the rupiah and bartering for goods is part of everyday life. Stall holders in the markets will be shocked if you don't try to strike a bargain with them.

## PLACES TO GO

**The National Monument**

### The National Monument in Merdeka Square

Commemorating Indonesia's struggle for independence, this 137-m obelisk was completed in 1975.

Jakarta Catholic Cathedral

### Istiqlal Mosque

This beautiful mosque is the largest place of worship for Muslims in South-east Asia and the fourth biggest mosque in the world. Around 120,000 worshippers can fit inside. It was finished in 1978 and commemorates the independence of Indonesia from the Dutch.

### Jakarta Catholic Cathedral

Indonesia is mostly a Muslim country, but in Jakarta the people are proud to embrace all religions. Facing the Istiqlal Mosque is the Jakarta Catholic Cathedral (above) which was completed in 1901. It has three spires and is built in the Gothic style, like many European cathedrals.

Istiqlal Mosque

# FOOD

### Street treats

Food in Jakarta has been influenced by its Chinese, Indian and European citizens. Nasi goreng, which means fried rice, is one of the most famous national dishes. Street vendors serve up anything from deep-fried yam or pineapple and fresh coconut milk, to sweet and savoury stuffed pancakes.

# THINGS TO DO

### Celebrate Indonesia's independence

On 17 August every year the people of Jakarta celebrate Independence Day. The celebrations include a flag-raising ceremony at the Presidential Palace in Jakarta. Colourful and noisy parades are another highlight.

### Visit a kampung

Jakarta is a modern city but many of its people live in simple bamboo and wooden homes in villages called kampungs. People move to the city to find work and have to make their own homes. They use whatever materials they can find. In some areas the people do not have clean water, electricity or good sanitation. Indonesia is prone to flooding and Jakarta is one of the fastest sinking cities in the world. Homes along the waterfront of the Ciliwung River are often flooded.

Kampung

Nearly half of the people living in Delhi live in slums where there is no access to fresh water, toilets or electricity. Slums have been built along the Yamuna river in the city. Poor sanitation and disease are a constant problem in these environments.

The **Qutub Minar** has been part of the Delhi skyline for around 1,000 years. It is 73 m tall and for many years people could climb all the way to the top. Sadly, in 1981, 47 people were crushed to death in a stampede as they tried to evacuate the tower, so now it is closed to the public.

The winding, crowded streets of **Old Delhi** are filled with people, shops and food vendors spilling onto the pavement. Cars, mopeds, rickshaws and bicycles are whizzing everywhere. It feels frenzied but friendly here!

The **Jama Masjid Mosque** was completed in 1656 and is one of the largest mosques in India. Its courtyard can hold 25,000 people.

**Delhi Metro**, the world's tenth-longest metro system, is the fastest way to travel across the city. It has six lines and a total of 214 stations. Every day it transports millions of passengers – often there's standing room only.

# DELHI
## INDIA

Welcome to Delhi, one of the busiest and most colourful cities in the world. The capital city of India has an estimated population of over 18 million. From the top of the Jama Masjid mosque you can see where New Delhi meets the old city.

**Connaught Place** is the most important financial, business and commercial area in New Delhi. It was built by British colonists in 1929 and has an underground shopping plaza as well as lush green areas.

The **Lotus Temple** is a Bahá'í House of Worship which means that people from any faith can pray here. It's shaped like a lotus flower and was opened in 1986. It is one of the most visited buildings in the entire world.

**Swaminarayan Akshardham** is the biggest Hindu temple in the city. Built from pink sandstone and cream marble, it looks like a magnificent ancient building, but it was actually completed in 2002.

## HISTORY

Delhi is one of the oldest capitals in the world and has been the centre of empires and kingdoms since ancient times. New Delhi was created by British colonists in 1911 and made the capital in 1931. India gained independence from the British in 1947. Since then this noisy, vibrant city has continued to expand.

## MONEY

**Mahatma Gandhi** (1869–1948) was an Indian lawyer who became a political activist and led a peaceful protest against British rule. His portrait regularly appears on the Indian rupee, the currency used in India.

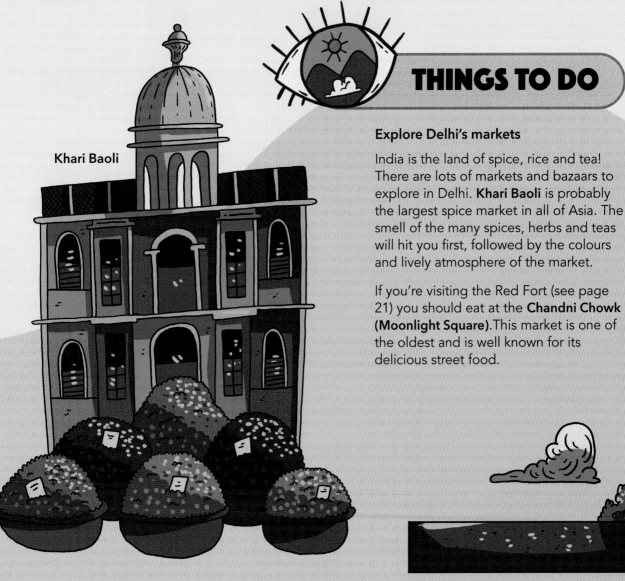

Khari Baoli

## THINGS TO DO

### Explore Delhi's markets

India is the land of spice, rice and tea! There are lots of markets and bazaars to explore in Delhi. **Khari Baoli** is probably the largest spice market in all of Asia. The smell of the many spices, herbs and teas will hit you first, followed by the colours and lively atmosphere of the market.

If you're visiting the Red Fort (see page 21) you should eat at the **Chandni Chowk (Moonlight Square)**. This market is one of the oldest and is well known for its delicious street food.

# FOOD

### Chickpea creativity

Check out chaat, a delicious snack made from potato, chickpeas and spices.

Another chickpea dish is **Chole bhature**. You can eat this fried bread and bean dish for breakfast washed down with a glass of **lassi** which is a kind of watered-down yoghurt drink.

Chole bhature

Chaat

# PLACES TO GO

### Birla House

Mahatma Gandhi lived out his final days in Delhi before he was assassinated in his garden at Birla House. A memorial marks the spot where he died and there is a museum in his old home.

### The Red Fort

The famous red sandstone building known as the Red Fort was built by the Mughal emperor Shah Jahan in 1639. This was the home of the mighty Mughals for around two hundred years.

Birla House

The Red Fort

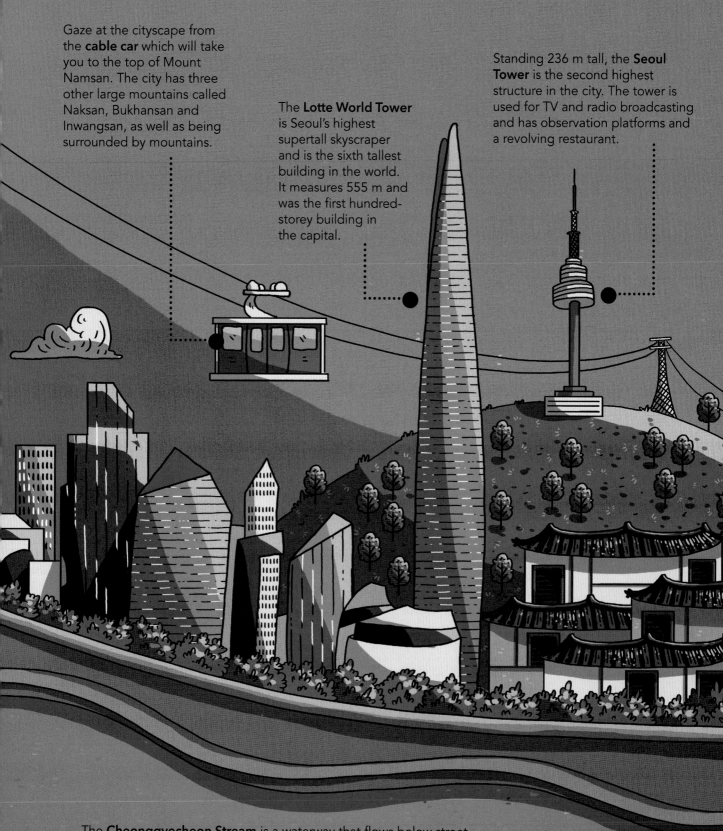

Gaze at the cityscape from the **cable car** which will take you to the top of Mount Namsan. The city has three other large mountains called Naksan, Bukhansan and Inwangsan, as well as being surrounded by mountains.

The **Lotte World Tower** is Seoul's highest supertall skyscraper and is the sixth tallest building in the world. It measures 555 m and was the first hundred-storey building in the capital.

Standing 236 m tall, the **Seoul Tower** is the second highest structure in the city. The tower is used for TV and radio broadcasting and has observation platforms and a revolving restaurant.

The **Cheonggyecheon Stream** is a waterway that flows below street level through many parts of the centre of Seoul. Over the years, the stream had largely been covered by concrete, but in 2005 the area was cleaned up, modernised and turned into an urban park.

One of the oldest neighbourhoods in the city is **Bukchon Hanok Village**. The traditional wooden homes are called hanoks. These were once the homes of important people, but many are now shops. A walk around these winding streets is like taking a trip into the past.

# SEOUL
## SOUTH KOREA

**Seoul, the capital of South Korea, is often called the 'miracle on the Han River'. It's one of the fastest developing cities in the world with a population of nearly 10 million. Asian culture meets Western ways in this lively city. There are old palaces and temples to explore, as well as exciting new art, fashion and music.**

Seoul has some of the best public transport systems in the world. The **Seoul Metropolitan Subway** is the most convenient way to get around. The service started in 1974 and is expanding to meet the needs of this growing city.

The **Banpo Bridge** is one of over thirty bridges built over the **Han River**. It is a double-deck bridge and its bottom deck is designed to submerge when the river rises. It's famous for its spectacular fountain which is the longest in the world and looks beautiful when it's lit up at night.

# HISTORY

People have lived beside the Han River in present-day Seoul since ancient times. The Joseon Dynasty ruled Korea for five centuries, from the end of the fourteenth century. They made Seoul the capital of Korea and built elegant royal palaces. Throughout its history the city has been fought over by foreign powers, including Japan and North Korea. Seoul became the capital of South Korea in 1948 and has been growing and developing its own style ever since.

## MONEY

The currency in use in Seoul is called the won.

Gwangjang Market

## THINGS TO DO

### Celebrate Buddha's birthday

**Buddhism** and **Christianity** are the main religions in South Korea. Religion is becoming less important to young people in Seoul, but Buddha's birthday is still widely celebrated and wonderful to watch. There are parades in the city and paper lanterns are hung everywhere.

### Experience K-Pop

In recent years there has been a new musical sensation called K-Pop. Seoul is a great place to experience this modern South Korean music. BTS are a famous boy band that formed in Seoul in 2013.

*Gangnam Style* by PSY was the first international K-Pop hit. There is a sculpture celebrating *Gangnam Style* outside the COEX mall – which happens to be the largest shopping mall in Asia.

*Gangnam Style* sculpture

# FOOD

### Korean BBQ

BBQ is popular all over South Korea, but the best bites around are in Seoul. Grilled dishes such as **Galbi (ribs)** or **samgyeopsal (pork belly)** are cooked at the table for you to eat.

### Kimbap and octopus

**Gwangjang Market** is a great place to try Korean food. This is one of the oldest markets in the city and has more than 5,000 shops. It's a good place to try **Kimbap**, which is similar to sushi rolls. Octopus is another delicacy on offer!

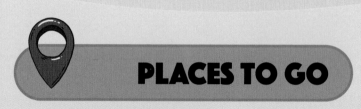

**Kimbap and octopus**

**Gyeongbokgung Palace**

# PLACES TO GO

### Gyeongbokgung Palace

Built in 1395, this was the first and largest royal residence in the city. The palace was burned down in the sixteenth century, but its halls and pavilions were rebuilt and have been beautifully restored. Children can play among the animal statues in the gardens.

### Changdeokgung Palace

This was the second royal palace. It was built in the early fifteenth century.

### Dongdaemun Design Plaza

Seoul has some exciting modern architecture. The Dongdaemun Design Plaza was designed by world-famous architect Zaha Hadid, and opened in 2014. Hadid was known as 'The Queen of the Curve' and this building shows why – it has no angles or straight lines. Inside there is a history museum and there are exhibitions about Korean product design.

### Jogyesa Buddhist Temple

This working temple is the centre of Zen Buddhism in Korea. It opened in 1910, although there has been a temple on the site since 1395. You'll see monks chanting, playing drums or meditating here.

**Dongdaemun Design Plaza**

The Alborz mountain range fringes the city. Its highest peak is **Mount Damavand** which is a dormant volcano and the highest mountain in Iran. Standing 5,671 m high, it is capped with snow for six to eight months of the year.

The **Tochal Telecabin** takes visitors up to the summit of Mount Tochal. This mountain stands at 3,933 m and has one of the world's highest ski resorts.

You need a head for heights in this city! **Milad Tower** is 435 m high and is among the tallest telecommunication towers in the world.

The spectacular **Azadi Tower** was built in 1971 to commemorate the 2,500th anniversary of the first Persian Empire. Looking like a pair of flared trousers, it is one of the city's most famous landmarks!

# TEHRAN
## IRAN

**Valiasr Street** is the 18-km road that runs from the north to the south of the city. To the north it's hilly with more modern buildings. In the south it's flatter with more historic buildings and poorer areas. Like all the roads in the city, it gets jammed with traffic. Sycamore trees line each side of the road.

How exciting is it to be in one of the highest cities in the world? To the north of Tehran lie the Alborz mountains and to the south there is a desert. Expect hot summers and icy winters with snow. The city of Tehran has a population of 8.7 million, making it the most populated city in Iran and Western Asia.

Builders have been adding to the **Mosalla Mosque Complex** since the 1990s. This enormous modern building covers 650,000 m² and has minarets that soar 230 m into the sky.

The **Golestan Palace** was once the seat of the Qajar dynasty. The beautiful halls and palaces on the complex were built during the eighteenth and nineteenth centuries.

# HISTORY

Tehran lies to the north of Iran. It has a long history, but didn't become the capital until 1796. In recent years there has been talk of moving the capital from Tehran. This is because the city has developed quickly since the 1920s, resulting in terrible air pollution. Tehran is also at risk of devastating earthquakes as it is on two geological fault lines.

## MONEY

In Tehran the currency in use is the Iranian rial.

**Treasury of National Jewels**

# PLACES TO GO

### Treasury of National Jewels

The magnificent Iranian crown jewels are on view at the Treasury of National Jewels at the Central Bank of the Islamic Republic of Iran. Some of the pieces are hundreds of years old and are encrusted with precious diamonds, rubies and emeralds. You'll see some of the largest cut diamonds in the world here, too.

### Niavaran Palace

Nature, art and history meet at this beautiful palace, which was once the home of the last shah of Iran. Tehran is a busy city, but the palace's gardens are peaceful and relaxing.

**Niavaran Palace**

**Metro**

## FOOD

### Tah-chin

Rice, kebabs and salads are popular in Tehran. One of the most famous dishes to try is tah-chin. It is also known as Persian baked rice cake and is made from rice, saffron, yoghurt and chicken.

### Shisha

Taking tea and coffee are popular pastimes in the city. Tea houses are popular with men who also like to smoke shisha (water-pipes). Meanwhile, the coffee shops are common hangouts for students.

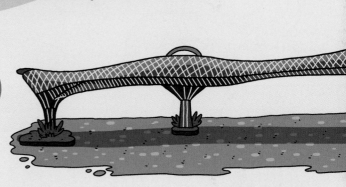

**Tah-chin**

**Shisha**

## THINGS TO DO

**Tabiat Bridge**

### Tabiat Bridge

One of the most unusual pedestrian bridges in the world, Tabiat Bridge connects two city parks and has three levels that follow a gentle S-shaped path. The levels are connected by ramps and stairways so there are many routes across the bridge. Opened in 2014, it was designed by architect Leila Araghian, and subsequently won her many awards.

### Shop in the Grand Bazaar

You can easily get lost on a shopping trip in the Tehran Grand Bazaar – it has 10 km of alleys and lanes to wander around! Most lanes specialise in certain goods, such as gold, paper, spices or carpets.

### Ride the metro

The Tehran metro is the fastest and cheapest way to get across the city. Women can choose to travel in female-only carriages.

**Tehran Grand Bazaar**

Only trains, mopeds, bicycles and pedestrians can use the historic **Long Bien Bridge**. It was built by the French and opened in 1902, but was badly damaged in 1967 and 1972 when it was bombed during the Vietnam War (1955-1975).

People can escape the noisy city at one of Hanoi's many lakes. At **Hoan Kiem Lake** in the Old Quarter (see page 31) you may spy one of the large, rare turtles. The Turtle Tower sits in the middle of the lake. At the northern end of the lake there is a little red bridge (Huc Bridge) which connects to the tiny Jade Island. In the centre of this island stands Ngoc Son Temple (Temple of the Jade Mountain).

The West Lake is the largest freshwater lake in the city. People often hire boats or eat in one of the floating restaurants. The magical-looking **Tran Quoc Pagoda** sits on an island in the lake. This Buddhist temple dates from the sixth century and is the oldest pagoda in Hanoi.

Hanoi is built on low-lying land on the **Red River delta**. The Red River gets its name from the red-brown silt that it carries and deposits in the fertile delta.

# HANOI
## VIETNAM

The **One Pillar Pagoda** was originally built between 1028 and 1054 but has since been rebuilt many times. The little wooden temple is shaped like a lotus flower as it grows out of the water.

In recent years, Hanoi has been growing upwards. In 2011 the **Keangnam Hanoi Landmark Tower** was opened. Standing at 350 m, it is the tallest building in Vietnam.

Hanoi or Ha Noi translates as 'the city in a bend of the river'. Hanoi is also called the 'city of lakes' and the 'Paris of the East'. This vibrant city has a population of over 7.7 million and has become one of the most popular tourist destinations in Asia.

The historic and commercial heart of Hanoi is called the **Old Quarter**. It has a long history going back a thousand years. Its busy streets are filled with quirky alleyways, historic temples and buzzing street markets. Watch out for the many mopeds whizzing by!

The **French Quarter** was built during the French occupation at the end of the nineteenth century. It has some fine colonial buildings, including the Museum of Vietnamese History and the Hoa Lo Prison, now converted into an apartment block and a prison museum respectively.

# HISTORY

In 2010 Hanoi celebrated its 1,000th birthday. In the beginning the city was called Thang Long and only became Hanoi in 1831. It hasn't always been the capital either, but from 1902 to 1953 it was the capital of French Indochina. Hanoi became the official capital of Vietnam in 1945 after a revolution against French rule.

**The Hanoi Ceramic Road**

# PLACES TO GO

### The Hanoi Ceramic Road

To celebrate its birthday the city commissioned a massive piece of street art. The Hanoi Ceramic Road is a colourful mosaic that runs for 6.5 km along the walls of the Red River. It tells the story of Vietnam in different styles and features works by children and local artists.

### The Temple of Literature

The site of the first university in Vietnam, the Temple of Literature was built, in 1070, to honour the Chinese philosopher Confucius (551–479 BCE). The peaceful courtyard and gardens and historic pavilion and temple buildings are built in a traditional Vietnamese style.

### Hanoi Opera House

This beautiful opera house stands in the centre of the city. It was built by French colonists in 1911 and was modelled on a famous opera house in Paris.

### Visit the Ho Chi Minh Mausoleum

There are always long queues of people wanting to visit Ho Chi Minh's body at the mausoleum to pay their respects to the former leader.

**The Temple of Literature**

**Hanoi Opera House**

**Ho Chi Minh Mausoleum**

# HANOI
## VIETNAM

## MONEY

Ho Chi Minh was the leader of the Republic of Vietnam from 1945 and is regarded as a hero in the country. He is affectionately known as Uncle Ho. His portrait is on the front of the Vietnamese **Dong**, the currency of the country.

## FOOD

**Pho**

In the Old Quarter there are lots of street vendors selling freshly cooked food like fried tofu and rice noodles. Hanoi is famous for a kind of noodle soup called Pho (say 'fuh'). Egg coffee is served, made with whisked egg yolk.

## THINGS TO DO

Pho

**Watch a water puppet show**

Water puppet shows are unique to Vietnam, and the **Thang Long Water Theatre** in Hanoi is the best place to see them. Water puppetry began in the eleventh century when villagers would perform shows on the flooded paddy rice fields. At Thang Long a pool of water is used as the stage. An orchestra plays traditional instruments, including wooden bells, bamboo flutes and drums, as the story is told. Puppeteers hidden behind a screen control the puppets with rods.

**Thang Long Water Theatre**

33

The impressive **Burj Khalifa** is the tallest building in the world by far! This giant tapering tower was finished in 2010. Its tip reaches 829.8 m into the sky and is sometimes hidden in the clouds. The highest part that you can visit is 584.5 m. The observation deck on the 124th floor gives you the best views of the city.

The awesome **Al Ittihad Bridge** is better known as the 'Dubai Smile' because of its massive steel arch that rises 100 m high. It has twelve lanes of traffic and two footpaths – the city has never been so connected!

**Dubai Creek** divides the city neatly in two. On the western side there is the historic district of Bur Dubai. Opposite is Deira, the commercial heart of the city.

Dubai is famous for its artificial islands that are built on land reclaimed from the Persian Gulf. The Palm Islands were started in 2001 and the **Palm Jumeirah** was the first to be inhabited in 2006. From the sky it looks like a giant palm tree. Houses, hotels, shops, beaches and luxury resorts have all been built on the reclaimed land.

The **Floating Bridge** connects Deira to the golf and yacht club. It was finished in 2007 and was only supposed to be temporary.

People still use traditional wooden taxi boats called abras to cross the Dubai Creek.

# DUBAI
## UNITED ARAB EMIRATES

Dubai and its many skyscrapers sparkle in the hot desert sunshine. This modern city is perched on the Persian Gulf coastline within the Arabian Desert. It is known as the 'city of gold' or the 'shopping capital of the Middle East'. The metropolis has a population of around three million. Each year, millions more flock here to enjoy luxury holidays.

Dubai is well known for its expensive, luxury hotels and restaurants. The **Burj Al Arab** hotel is one of the top hotels in the world. You can't miss it as it looks like the billowing sail of a ship, and stands on a small triangular artificial island. A double room can cost over £2,000 a night, but you will be served by a butler and the TVs are decorated with gold!

The beautiful **Jumeirah Mosque** stands to the north of **Dubai Marina**. This white sandstone building with its dome and minarets looks medieval, but it was only finished in 1979.

# HISTORY

Over 5,000 years ago the area that is now Dubai was under the sea. Then the sea receded, leaving the golden desert sands on which Dubai was built. In the early days of its history, nomadic people passed through the area, and there are records of traders stopping here en route to Iran. By the eighteenth century it was growing as a fishing settlement. Later the pearl industry boomed. However, it wasn't until the 1960s, and the discovery of oil, that modern Dubai began to develop. Now the oil has nearly gone, but tourism and recreation are making Dubai bigger and busier than ever.

# MONEY

People use the Arab Emirate Dirham in Dubai.

# PLACES TO GO

**The Dubai World Trade Centre**

One of the first skyscrapers in the city, the Dubai World Trade Centre was finished in 1979 and has hosted millions of visitors.

**Al Fahidi Fort**

Al Fahidi Fort is the oldest surviving building in the city. It dates from 1781 and today it houses the Dubai Museum.

**The Dubai Fountain**

This water feature, located on Burj Khalifa Lake, is the world's largest dancing fountain. Water shoots 152 m into the air as music plays.

Dubai World Trade Centre

The Dubai Fountain

Al Fahidi Fort

## THINGS TO DO

### Shop in the world's largest malls

Shopping is big business in Dubai and it has some of the smartest and largest malls in the world. Ibn Battuta Mall, named after an intrepid medieval explorer, is the biggest themed shopping mall in the world. It is themed around the places Ibn Battuta travelled to and has many well-known stores including Marks & Spencer, Debenhams and Decathlon.

With over 1,200 shops, the Dubai Mall is the biggest shopping mall in the world. It has all the top designer stores, including Chanel, Gucci and Dior. It also features an enormous aquarium! This has a 270-degree walk-through tunnel to get you up-close to the aquarium's inhabitants!

**Dubai trolley**

### Visit a market

Dubai is also home to lots of traditional markets (souks) selling spices, textiles, perfumes and gold.

### Take a tram trip

Take a trip around downtown on the Dubai trolley. These double-decker trams look old but they are modern and only started running in 2015. All trips are free!

**Dubai traditional market**

Bangkok is situated on the **Chao Phraya (the 'River of Kings') delta.** The great river runs through the city in a southerly direction and connects to a network of canals that will take you all over the city.

**Wat Phra Kaew (the Temple of the Emerald Buddha)** is situated within the grounds of the Grand Palace. This is the most important Buddhist temple in Thailand and the statue of the Emerald Buddha is the most revered religious icon in the land. Everyone who visits the temple should dress respectfully and remove their shoes.

**Rattanakosin Island** is the heart of old Bangkok. The Grand Palace which was built in 1782, is located on the island. The king of Thailand lived here until 1925 and it is still used for some official ceremonies.

Before roads were built in the nineteenth century the **Chao Phraya** was the best way to travel across the city – for this reason it was called the 'Venice of the East'. The river is quieter these days but it's still a great way for tourists to see the main attractions. Many of the great temples are located along the banks of the river.

# BANGKOK
## THAILAND

Bangkok is a growing city. There are 581 skyscrapers over 90 m tall.

Welcome to Bangkok, the capital city of Thailand! This bright, friendly and super-busy city is also known as the 'City of Angels' (from the Thai name Krung Thep) but it could easily be called the city of Buddhas for its many temples and statues. It has a population of over eight million and is the most visited city in the world.

**King Power MahaNakhon** (also known as Pixel Tower) was the tallest building in the city until 2018. It stands at 314.2 m in the financial district of the city.

**ICONSIAM** is a new building on the Bangkok skyline. This skyscraper stands next to the Chao Phraya River and its Tower 1 is the tallest building in the city. The ICONSIAM shopping mall opened in 2018. The massive pane of pleated glass along the front of the mall is the largest of its kind in the world.

Bangkok has developed quickly since the 1960s. Sadly, there are urban slums everywhere in this city. **Khlong Toei** is one of the worst for poverty and crime. Many of the ramshackle wooden homes here have tin roofs and are built on stilts beside the polluted waters of the river.

# HISTORY

In the fifteenth century a village grew up alongside the Chao Phraya River. In 1782 the king, Rama I, moved the Thai capital there and Bangkok was born. King Rama I built temples and the Grand Palace at Rattanakosin Island. Trade with China and later Europe helped the city to grow. Today Bangkok is a mixture of the old and the new. Amongst all the skyscrapers and shopping malls there are some beautiful old parts of the city to enjoy.

# MONEY

The Thai baht is the currency used in Bangkok.

**Temple of the Reclining Buddha**

# PLACES TO GO

**The Temple of the Reclining Buddha**

Most people in Thailand are Buddhists and Bangkok has some of the most spectacular Buddhist temples. The Temple of the Reclining Buddha (Wat Pho) is home to a 46-m-long Buddha that shimmers with gold leaf.

**Temple of Dawn**

The colourful spires of the Temple of Dawn (Wat Arun) are majestic and magical.

**Wat Traimit**

The largest solid gold Buddha in the world sits within the temple of Wat Traimit.

**Wat Arun**

# FOOD

### Patonggo and ba mee

Yaowarat Road in Chinatown is one of the oldest parts of the city and the place to sample lovely street food, including *patonggo* (fried dough sticks) or the noodle dish *ba mee*.

Patonggo

### Chatuchak Weekend market

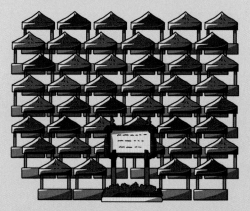

# THINGS TO DO

### Shop in Chatuchak weekend market

You can buy just about anything at this market in eastern Bangkok. It has over 8,000 market stalls, selling everything from pets to plastic Buddhas. It is easily the biggest market in the country but it is organised into different sections so you should find what you're looking for!

### Relax in Lumpini Park

Bangkok life is fast and frantic but you can escape to leafy quiet areas. Lumpini Park is filled with palm trees and other exotic tropical plants. Down by the lake you may bump into a water monitor lizard. They can swim and run fast and may bite, so make sure you leave them alone!

### Ride in a tuk tuk

Tuk tuks have become a symbol for Thailand. In Bangkok you'll see these open-air, three-wheeled vehicles whizzing everywhere.

Tuk tuk

Water monitor lizard

41

Hong Kong is situated on the Pearl River estuary. It is made up of 263 islands, but the main parts are Hong Kong Island, Kowloon Peninsula, the New Territories and Lantau Island.

To the west of Hong Kong Island is **Victoria Peak** (also known as Mount Austin). This hill is 552 m high and you'll get a great view of the entire city and Victoria Harbour from here. The old **Peak Tram** is the best way to get to the top.

The **International Commerce Centre** is 484 m high, making it the tallest building in Hong Kong.

There isn't much room left in Hong Kong, which is why they like to build upwards! In 2019 there were 317 high-rises taller than 150 m in the city.

**Wan Chai** is a fascinating and historic part of Hong Kong. It has lots to see with its British-style, colonial buildings, temples, street markets, restaurants, bars and old-style housing.

You can travel across **Victoria Harbour** on the green and white **Star Ferry**.

# HONG KONG

## CHINA

The hot and hectic city of Hong Kong is found on the south coast of China. This neon-lit city is an important financial and commercial centre and has more skyscrapers than anywhere else in the world. It's home to over 7.4 million people but the population density, at 6,765 people per km², is very high so the city can feel very crowded.

**Lantau Island** is at the mouth of the Pearl River. It is green and mountainous and it's where you will find the epic **Tian Tan Buddha**. This 34 m-high statue is the largest outdoor-seated Buddha in the world. You need to climb 268 steps to reach the statue but you will be rewarded with stunning views.

Wan Chai also has modern buildings, such as the **Hong Kong Convention and Exhibition Centre** which stands proud on the waterfront.

Far away from the busy city is Lantau's 200-year-old **Tai O fishing village**. Here you can see traditional bamboo houses on stilts. There are also semi-floating markets selling seafood.

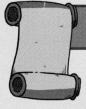
# HISTORY

Hong Kong has been inhabited by humans since ancient times. Originally it was a small fishing town, but its position on the Pearl River made it an important port of call for ships trading between Asia and the Middle East and a gateway to China. The Chinese city fell into British hands in 1841. It remained part of the British Empire until 1997, when the city was handed back to China. Hong Kong may be part of China, but for now it is mostly free to make its own rules about how it is run. There have been clashes between police and anti-government protestors demonstrating against moves to curb this independence.

# MONEY

The currency in Hong Kong is the HK dollar, but you don't need to travel with loads of cash. You can use a smartcard called the Octopus to pay for travel, groceries or even fast food. The Octopus also comes as a small chip which can be worn like a charm on a bracelet.

**Ten Thousand Buddhas Monastery**

# PLACES TO GO

### Tang Ancestral Hall

Dating back to 1271, Tang Ancestral Hall is one of the oldest buildings in the city.

### Flagstaff House Museum

Flagstaff House Museum is a typical British colonial building. It was completed in 1846 and was the home for the commander of the British army. Now it is a museum  for tea.

**Tang Ancestral Hall**

Drinking tea is a tradition in China and this is a good place to learn all about it!

### Ten Thousand Buddhas Monastery

This monastery, with its striking crimson pagoda, looks like a place built long ago. Actually, it was finished in 1957, it isn't a working monastery and nor does it have 10,000 Buddhas – it has around 13,000 statues all striking a different pose!

### Kowloon Walled City

For much of the twentieth century, the Kowloon Walled City was a no-go area. It was overcrowded and run by criminal gangs. The whole area was demolished in 1994 and the Kowloon Walled City Park was created in its place. Now it's a peaceful place with beautifully designed gardens. Many people come here to practise the martial art of Tai Chi.

# FOOD

**Try a taste of paradise**

Hong Kong is so famous for its food that it has been described as a 'gourmet paradise'. Many dishes have a strong Chinese or British influence. Noodles and rice are always on the menu. Street foods including dim sum (small bite-sized dishes such as dumplings and sesame balls), egg waffles and fish balls are popular, too. Fried pig intestines, organs (innards of animals) in a pot and fermented tofu are definitely dishes for the more adventurous!

Dim sum

# THINGS TO DO

**See the Sevens**

The Hong Kong Sevens is a famous rugby tournament that takes place in the city in March or April every year. People travel from all over the world to watch the event and join in the party atmosphere that takes over the city.

**The Hong Kong Sevens**

**Travel by tram**

A great way to travel around Hong Kong is by tram. People call these old-fashioned double-decker trams 'ding dings' in reference to the sound of a bell that warns of their approach. You hop on the back, then pay as you exit from the front of the tram.

Ding dings

# MORE ASIAN CITIES

## ISLAMABAD (PAKISTAN)

Islamabad only became the capital of Pakistan in 1966. It is a planned city and has a grid plan with wide avenues and plenty of green spaces. Modern meets traditional Islamic style in this city.

**Population:** 1,014,825 (2017)

**Highest building:** Telecom Tower 113 m

**Places to see:** Faisal Mosque, Star and Crescent Monument, Pakistan Monument

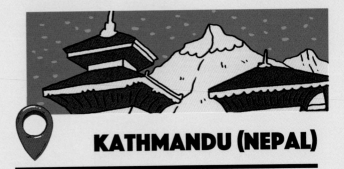

## KATHMANDU (NEPAL)

High up in the Himalayan hills (at around 1,400 m) is Kathmandu, the capital city of Nepal. It's known as the City of Temples for its many Buddhist and Hindu temples. The city was severely damaged in a massive earthquake in 2015, but is slowly being rebuilt.

**Population:** 985,000 (2019)

**Highest building:** Silver City Apartments 68.18 m

**Places to see:** Swayambhunath Temple ('Monkey Temple'), Durbar Square, Jagannath Mandir, Royal Palace

## MANILA (PHILIPPINES)

Manila, the capital city of the Philippines, is the most densely populated city in the world. It is also known as the 'Pearl of the Orient'. It has been damaged by earthquakes and wars, but is now a buzzing, modern city.

**Population:** 1,780,148 (2015)

**Highest building:** Federal Land Tower 318 m

**Places to see:** Rizal Park, Fort Santiago, San Agustin Church, Federal Land Tower

## SINGAPORE CITY (SINGAPORE)

This is one of the richest cities in the world with some of the best restaurants, top shops and cleanest streets you'll ever see. It is built on an island and there are modern and old parts of the city to explore, including its own Little India and Chinatown.

**Population:** 5,814,004 (2019)

**Highest building:** Guoco Tower 290 m

**Places to see:** Sri Veeramakaliamman temple, Singapore Botanic Gardens, Tanjong Pagar Centre

# SHANGHAI (CHINA)

The largest city in China is also the busiest container port in the world. The old world meets the modern one in this fast-developing city on the Yangtze River Delta. This is the financial and commercial centre of China and boasts a magnificent skyline of epic skyscrapers.

**Population**: 26,317,104 (2019)

**Highest building:** Shanghai Tower 632 m

**Places to see:** Songjiang Square Pagoda, the Old City of Shanghai, Mahavira Hall

# RIYADH, SAUDI ARABIA

Riyadh is the political, financial and commercial hub of Saudi Arabia and one of the wealthiest places in the world. This city in the desert has had a massive growth spurt since the 1950s.

**Population:** 7,676,654 (2018)

**Highest building:** Burj Rafal 307.9 m

**Places to see:** Masmak Fortress, King Abdullah Park, Centerpoint, Burj Al Faisaliyah

# ANKARA, TURKEY

Ankara took over from Istanbul as the capital of Turkey in 1923. There are many ancient and archaeological sites to see, but Ankara is also a thriving modern city. Angora wool (from rabbits, goats and cats in the region) takes its name from the city.

**Population:** 5,445,026

**Highest building:** Merkez Ankara Office Tower 301 m

**Places to see:** Mausoleum of Mustafa Kemal Atatürk, Ankara Castle and the Citadel in the Old Quarters, Kocatepe Mosque

# DHAKA, BANGLADESH

The capital city of Bangladesh is also known as 'the rickshaw capital of the world'. The city has ancient roots with a history of Mughal and British rule. It only became the capital in 1971. Now it is a busy place with old sections and well-planned modern areas to explore.

**Population:** 8,906,039

**Highest building:** City Centre Dhaka 171 m

**Places to see:** Ahsan Manzil, Lalbagh Fort, Jatiya Sangsad Bhaban, Star Mosque, Dhakeshwari Temple

# GLOSSARY

**assassination**
the killing of someone for a political reason.

**colony**
an area under the control of another country.

**delta**
a large, triangular area at the mouth of a river.

**dynasty**
a line of related people who rule a country.

**geological**
relating to geology – the study of the Earth's structure and what it is made from.

**Gothic**
a style of architecture used for important buildings from the twelfth to the sixteenth century.

**mausoleum**
a building that contains the remains of dead people.

**medieval**
relating to the Middle Ages (600 - 1500).

**metropolis**
a large and important city.

**minaret**
a tower attached to a mosque.

**monument**
a structure built to celebrate an important person or event.

**obelisk**
a tall, four-sided monument.

**occupation**
a time when one country stays in another country and controls it by force.

**republic**
a country that is run by the people rather than hereditary rulers such as kings and queens.

**revolution**
the overthrow of a government.

**silt**
very fine sand or clay that is carried by water.

**Tai Chi**
a Chinese martial art.

# INDEX